TAKE A LESSON IN
ENGLISH

TAKE A LESSON IN

ENGLISH

by Barbara Murray B. A., M. A. (Hons)., M. Sc.

W. FOULSHAM & CO. LIMITED
LONDON • NEW YORK • TORONTO • CAPE TOWN • SYDNEY

W. Foulsham & Co. Limited
The Publishing House, Bennetts Close
Cippenham, Berks SL1 5AP, England

ISBN 0-572-02171-2

Note: Some of this material was originally published in the
book *English Lessons At A Moment's Notice*

Printed in Great Britain by The Bath Press, Bath.

Acknowledgements

The author and publisher are grateful for
permission to reproduce the following:

DULCE ET DECORUM EST
The estate of Wilfred Owen and Publishers
Chatto & Windus: The Hogarth Press. (Page 71).

A DISSERTATION UPON ROAST
PIG by Charles Lamb from *Essays of Elia*
(Everyman's Library) published by J. M. Dent.
(Page 77).

BRER RABBIT, THE ELEPHANT
AND THE WHALE from *101 School
Assembly Stories* by Frank Carr, published by
W. Foulsham & Co. Ltd. (Page 81).

Contents

Introduction

This book is about English in all its forms: the written and the spoken; poetry and prose; sentences, phrases and words.

But it is not a text book. It is intended for teachers who will have to take over at a moment's notice without the luxury of time to prepare materials and choose extracts for study. Accordingly, each unit has been designed so that the only aids required are a board and chalk (or their equivalents) for the teacher, and pencils and paper for the students.

The units themselves are a series of suggestions for 'one off' lessons which may or may not have any follow-up; thus mountains of marking for the relieving and the returning teacher are avoided. Above all, it is hoped that the lessons will be seen as imaginative, positive and often entertaining. (There is no logical reason why learning should ever be dull.) This will help to alleviate the problems that accompany the teaching of an unfamiliar class by an unfamiliar teacher in an unaccustomed role. The teacher's function here is seen as that of a guide to the discovery of new ways through old mazes.

The units are designed to be practical in nature so that pupils will 'learn through doing' and thus be helped on their way to a fuller understanding of the workings and power of words.

To develop a mastery of the language, the pupil must develop a way of looking at things accurately, of experiencing things fully, and of expressing things clearly.

It is hoped that the creative acts demanded of the pupils will enable them to do this; thus they will learn to make decisions, select ideas, and bring critical capacities into play.

All the units are directly or indirectly based on exercises and activities which pupils have been found to enjoy. The author knows them to be workable and effective for pupils through a range of ages and abilities, giving an outlet for self-expression which sometimes, seemingly, has no direct relevance to native intelligence.

To facilitate the choosing of material, all units have level indicators denoting relative complexity of the material to be used. *Level A* is intended to be a simpler exercise; *Level B* a more complex one; while *Level C* is for more able or advanced pupils. It is important to remember, however, that *grading is a relative exercise*. The final choice of level and material must be left to the judgement of the teacher. The ideas presented could be adapted further to suit a particular class or need; in that case they will form the basis for other imaginative work and presentations.

The units themselves are divided thematically into 5 sections, each based on one particular skill, followed by some classroom quizzes.

1.   FUN WITH WORDS deals with *vocabulary building* and word power.

2.   TALK IT OUT involves *guided discussion*.

3.   SOLVE THIS ONE comprises *problem-solving* units.

4.   EVERYONE'S A WRITER aims to build confidence in *writing creatively*, both in poetry and prose.

5.   SHAKESPEARE SHAKE-OUT focuses on universal themes and conditions in *play interpretations*.

The units are worded for the teacher, giving a *suggested level* and *class organisation* (both of which will depend on the class make-up and on the strengths and style of the individual teacher), an *introductory comment* to establish the content of the unit, and *instructions on the running* of the unit. Materials to be written on the board are listed clearly and answers are given to all exercises.

Because of the nature of the book, the units are not intended to be linked sequentially in any way. They are simply a series of individual lessons, grouped under thematic headings, which will cover a 40 minute period. Thus they can be dipped into at random. Where feedback sessions are indicated, these can be as long or short as the teacher finds necessary. Some units suggest possibilities for further work or follow up at home.

At the end of the book there is a work sheet on which can be recorded those units that have been used by the different classes. This could be helpful to Relief teachers who may not know the 'history' of the classes they are meeting.

Fun with Words

Vocabulary study

1   CRISSCROSS   (Levels A, B & C)

1   Divide the class into groups of 3 or 4.

2   Ask the pupils to give you *any* 5 words they can think of off the tops of their heads. You might get one word from each group. (These words should not seem to be related.)

     e.g.   POLICEMAN   SUNSHINE   ANXIETY SENSITIVE   MOUNTAIN

3   Write the words on the board in the following pattern, as they are fired at you:

POLICEMAN   SENSITIVE

                  ANXIETY

SUNSHINE   MOUNTAIN

4   Giving the groups *10 minutes maximum*, ask the pupils to make word associations diagonally. They should start in the corners and work towards the centre till it is seen that each of the corner words is linked with the centre word.

A finished example might look like this:

POLICEMAN   SENSITIVE

patrol   appearance

robbers   jokes

guns

ANXIETY

cancer   climbers

sunburn   avalanche

snowstorm

SUNSHINE   MOUNTAIN

5   After the time is up, have the groups compare their creations.
    These could be read out, written on the board by you, or, with a
    small number of groups, one 'scribe' for each group could write
    the contributions on the board.

6   Begin subsequent rounds with further sets of 5 words from the
    groups.

If you know beforehand that the pupils you are to take have been
studying specific words in class or for homework, you could give a
selection of 5 words from these lists to start the game off.
    An element of competition can be built into the game by seeing
which group can create the longest list of associations before reaching
the word in the centre.

2   A CACOPHONY OF SOUND   (Levels A & B)

The following exercise may be attempted individually, in pairs or in
small groups. It encourages precision of thought, and the finding of
exact words to describe the sounds that animals make.

Creatures have voices which can make sounds that we think of as typical of each animal or bird. For example, when someone mentions the word FROG, you might say the word CROAK describes the typical sound it makes, whereas with the word DOG, you might say it typically BARKS.

1   Ask the pupils to see how many different words they can think of to describe the following animals.

LEVEL A
ASS (bray)
BEE (hum/buzz)
BULL (bellow)
CAT (purr)
HORSE (neigh)
LAMB (bleat)
PIG (grunt)
SNAKE (hiss)
OWL (hoot)
PIGEON (coo)

LEVEL B
COW (low)
HYENA (scream)
MONKEY (chatter)
HEN (cackle/cluck)
TURKEY (gobble)
ELEPHANT (trumpet)
CROW (caw)
WOLF (howl)
SWALLOW (twitter)
ROBIN (chirp)

2   Now ask the pupils to see how many different words they can think of which describe the ways these animals move.

ASS (trot   SNAKE (glide)   HEN (strut)
BEE (flit)   OWL (flit)   LAMB (frisk/gambol)
BULL (charge)   PIGEON (flutter)   CROW (flap)
CAT (slink)   TURKEY (strut)   WOLF (lope)
HORSE (gallop)   COW (wander)   SWALLOW (dive)
ELEPHANT (amble)   HYENA (prowl)   ROBIN (hop)
PIG (trot)   MONKEY (scramble)

3 MAGIGRAPHS   (Levels A, B & C)

This exercise encourages freedom of structure in writing by experimentation with form. Pupils can work individually, or in pairs.

The idea is to choose a subject that can be conveyed in an optical and original design, but using words and phrases to create the shapes required.

The content of the writing should be sensible, and appropriate to the shape being created.

To provide inspiration, you could create a 'magigraph' on the board with the help of the class.

Take, for example, the idea of *AN UMBRELLA*.

Ask the class for simple words or phrases that they think describe an umbrella well. Write the words in a list on the board. Your list might look like this:

rainbow colours	joyful
silk	wet slopes
protection	glisten
shelter	bobbing
happy	

Now, using these words as your tools, create the shape of an umbrella. (You may want the pupils to help you fit the words together.) **See pages 16 and 17 for illustrations.**

Some further suggestions for subjects could be:

The Mouse

Man

The Sun

A Bus

A Spring Flower

A Cloud

A Happy Home

An Unhappy Home

With more advanced students, or the more sensitive and perceptive, it might be worthwhile to try one or two abstract ideas, e.g. Happiness, Growing Up, or even God.

It will be interesting to see what 'shape' is given to these ideas by the more imaginative young people.

rainbow colours,   silken slopes

protecting, joyfully bobbing, glistening

our shelter in a storm

Another example takes the idea of *THE DEAD TREE*.

wind shrieks through naked arms

the life that was

of the

a skeleton

the lonely sentinel stands

the last of the old guard

gnarled fingers twist skywards

Note Here we are using clauses and sentences rather than phrases.

Have the pupils choose their own subjects and write their own 'magigraphs'.

This exercise can be used to help build a more colourful vocabulary. It can be done in pairs or small groups.

Part (a) should be attempted without a dictionary; part (b) is a little more testing and therefore dictionaries should be used. You may also like to give the first letter of the correct answer to aid the search.

PART (a)

We sometimes use the habits of animals or birds to describe specific actions in human beings, e.g. the person who *boasts* could be described by the verb *to crow*.

Ask the pupils to see if they can find the *verbs* from the names of animals or birds, which could be used to describe the following actions:

following or pursuing	(to dog)
tracking someone down	(to hound)
mimicking in an unkind way	(to ape)
worrying or harassing	(to badger)
dipping or diving out of harm's way	(to duck)
seeking something out	(to ferret)
confusing or bewildering	(to fox)
crashing into something deliberately	(to ram)
eating greedily	(to wolf)
seeking opinions in an indirect way	(to fish)

PART (b)

We also like to use adjectives which come from Latin words for animals or birds and which describe characteristics associated with those creatures, e.g. elephant – ELEPHANTINE – enormous.

Ask the pupils to see how many other – INE adjectives they can find from the following creatures:

like an EAGLE	(aquiline)
like an ASS	(asinine)
like a DOG	(canine)
like a CAT	(feline)
like a LION	(leonine)
like a FOX	(vulpine)
like a HORSE	(equine)
like a COW/OX	(bovine)

like a WILD BEAST   (ferine)
like a FISH   (piscine)

Can the class use these adjectives in phrases or sentences?
e.g. He has an aquiline nose.

5 WORD TEASERS (Levels A, B & C)

This activity is best done individually or in pairs. Write the teasers on the board as set out below,

Example

```
┌─────────────────────┐
│     STAND           │
│    ───────          │
│       I             │
│                     │
│  I UNDERSTAND       │
└─────────────────────┘
```

and get the pupils to work out what they really mean (each could be a word or a phrase).

1
 	
       S
       K
       C
       O
PULL   S
	2 SOCIETY	**3**
		
		   AN
		———
		COAT

4
 	
   R
   O
ROADS
   D
   S
	5
	
	WE'RE
	———
	WORKED
		6
		
		  1
		———
		OTHER

7 WEATHER ——— HE'S	**8** SI HE'S DE	**9** LIVING ——— SHOESTRING

10
 	
SDRAW
	11
	
	———RU_N
		12
		
		  S
		  R
		  I
		  A
		  T
		  S

13
 	
C LION
   LION
   LION
	14
	
	CYCLE
	CYCLE
		15
		
		TIME/TIME

1 ME / LOOK	2 LIVING ‾‾‾‾‾ C C C C	3 I I I I
4 SIDE / SIDE	5 YOU'RE ‾‾‾‾‾ BALL	6 FEET FEET FEET FEET FEET FEET
7 OUTSIDE	8 MAKE ENDSSDNE	9 MEN MEN MEN MEN

10
 	
‾‾‾‾‾‾‾
READING
	11
	
	    D
	    E
	I'M F
		12
		
		INTEREST RATE

13
 	
SHE'S
‾‾‾‾‾
MOON
	14
	
	NRUT
		15 ANT
		    ANT
		    ANT
		    ANT ANT
		    ANT ANT
		           ANT
		           ANT
		           ANT

1 IT ÷ LOOK	**2** $$\frac{\text{M.A. PH.D}}{\text{O}}$$	**3** J T RIGHT U S
4 E D I S	**5** SO WE'RE UP	**6** $$\frac{\text{TAKER}}{\text{THE}}$$
7 OTHER /1	**8** P U	**9** BIDS BIDS BIDS BIDS
10 B lo O ok O ing K	**11** J U U S S T	**12** MACTERIAL
13 R T ☐ O O	**14** $$\frac{\text{I}}{\text{ESTIMATED}}$$	**15** OR OR OR OR OR OR OR OR OR OR

ANSWERS

LEVEL A		LEVEL B		LEVEL C	
1	Pull your socks up	1	Look after me	1	Look into it
2	High Society	2	Living overseas	2	Two degrees above zero
3	An overcoat	3	Eyes right!	3	Just about right
4	Crossroads	4	Side by Side	4	Right side up
5	We're overworked	5	You're on the ball	5	We're in the soup
6	One on top of the other	6	Six Feet tall/high	6	The undertaker
7	He's under the weather	7	Left outside	7	One after the other
8	He's inside	8	Make ends meet	8	Backup
9	Living on a shoestring	9	Foremen	9	Forbids
10	Backwards	10	Reading between the lines	10	Looking through the book
11	Run over	11	I'm fed up	11	Just between us
12	Upstairs	12	Low interest rate	12	See-through material
13	Sealions	13	She's over the moon	13	Square root
14	Bicycle	14	Turn back	14	I overestimated you
15	Time and time again	15	Tenants	15	Tenors

FOLLOW-UP
Now have the pupils create their own teasers.

6 HOMOPHONES (Levels A, B & C)

The following exercise may be done individually, in pairs or in small groups.

Many words in English sound the same but are spelt differently. The following groups of definitions all involve such confusions.

1   Write the pairs of definitions on the board for the pupils to work on to find the homophones (explain the word).

2   Insist on the correct spelling of the two words involved. A time limit may be set to give the more able students a challenge. You may wish to have groups compete to be the first to finish.

Each correctly chosen and spelt word scores a point.
Dictionaries may be allowed if they are available.

LEVEL A   Group 1

		Answers	
naked	an animal	bare	bear
to strike	a vegetable	beat	beet
a great price	an animal	dear	deer
soft hair	a tree	fur	fir
to run away	an insect	flee	flea
a title	darkness	knight	night
large	part of a fire-place	great	grate
did hear	a group of cows	heard	herd
speed of ships	no	knot	not
rest	a part	peace	piece

LEVEL A   Group 2   *Answers*

a series or collection	of pleasant taste	suite	sweet
way or style	a large estate	manner	manor
a town	to bore a hole	borough	burrow

(admit – not quite homophones)

part of a room	sticking down with wax	ceiling	sealing
made from corn	belonging to a series	cereal	serial
a group which makes decisions	to give advice	council	counsel
a shellfish	part of the body	mussel	muscle
gain	a person who foretells events	profit	prophet
a worker underground	a person under age	miner	minor
rose high	a fighting weapon	soared	sword

LEVEL A   Group 3   *Answers*

what you do with a book	a hollow stalk	read	reed
a circle	to twist	ring	wring
part of the ocean	to observe	sea	see
looks at long and hard	a series of steps	stares	stairs
something told	part of an animal	tale	tail
not strong	seven days	weak	week
couple	kind of fruit	pair	pear
use up foolishly	part of the body	waste	waist
the cost of a journey	just	fare	fair
post	masculine	mail	male

LEVEL B   Group 1   *Answers*

the full number	to praise	complement	compliment
the centre of a nut	commander of a regiment	kernel	colonel
chief	a basic truth	principal	principle
a short oar	bones of the head	scull	skull
a type of sign	a musical instrument	symbol	cymbal
to agree to	the act of going up	assent	ascent
made beer	a bird's offspring	brewed	brood
a cleft in the rock	one who harvests the sea	fissure	fisher
one who puts seed in the ground	one who uses a needle	sower	sewer
a special group in India	to throw	caste	cast

LEVEL B   Group 2   *Answers*

a member of the onion family	to let water in or out	leek	leak
a small thing	power	mite	might
a sound of distress	cut down	moan	mown
a bucket	with not much colour	pail	pale
to stop briefly	soft feet of an animal	pause	paws
to ask for urgently	the victim of a hunt	pray	prey
to fly upwards	painful	soar	sore
did fly	a kind of chimney	flew	flue
the noise a horse makes	no (archaic)	neigh	nay
a sheet of glass	ache	pane	pain

LEVEL B   Group 3

		Answers	
a covering for the head	fast running animal	hair	hare
to cry out	a spherical toy	bawl	ball
the sea shore	a tree	beach	beech
not fine	an area for racing	coarse	course
early morning wetness on grass	what is owing	dew	due
the front	the square of two	fore	four
has got bigger	a sound indicating pain	grown	groan
part of the foot	to cure	heel	heal
a kind of deer	vital part of the body	hart	heart
what is lent	alone	loan	lone

LEVEL C   Group 1

		Answers	
want	to work dough	need	knead
to peel	a fruit	pare	pear
empties out	holes in the skin	pours	pores
to knock	to enclose in paper	rap	wrap
proud	a blood vessel	vain	vein
a valley	a cover for the face	vale	veil
rind or skin	a ring of bells	peel	peal
a churchyard tree	a female sheep	yew	ewe
used to propel a boat	metal in its natural state	oar	ore
part of a circle	a biblical vessel	arc	ark

LEVEL C   Group 2

		Answers	
strong beer	to be unwell	ale	ail
what we breathe	one who inherits	air	heir
a tusked animal	to make a hole	boar	bore
a branch	to bend down	bough	bow
a position	to summon	site	cite
to lose life	to stain	die	dye
a measurement of length	a trick	feet	feat
dirty	a bird	foul	fowl
to cut	a colour	hew	hue
a male person	a sacred song	him	hymn

LEVEL C   Group 3

		Answers	
to pierce	a dress ornament	broach	brooch
makes tea	a pressure mark	brews	bruise
the inner part	a body of soldiers	core	corps
destiny	a feast or fair	fate	fête
to adorn with gold	a society for mutual aid	gild	guild
to think	stables	muse	mews
a fruit	a lead weight at the end of a line	plum	plumb
24 sheets of paper	a band of singers	quire	choir
what is sown	to give up	seed	cede
steps over a fence	manner	stile	style

This activity is best done by individuals or pairs. Each of the following words has more than one meaning. Which meaning is intended depends on the different functions the word has in any sentence. For example, the word may both describe something, and be an action word or verb:

a pérfect day

He perféct his grammar.

Such words can be easily distinguished in spoken English because the placing of the stress changes with the function of the word:

a pérfect example

He perféct his service at tennis.

In writing, these changes are not so easy to show, except by the context in which the word is used.

Now, see if you can show, by composing sentences, that we change the functions (and the pronunciation) of the following words. (*You will need to write two sentences for each word.*)

LEVEL A	LEVEL B	LEVEL C
Perfect	Contract	Defect
Content	Desert	Affix
Produce	Frequent	Discount
Insult	Escort	Recount
Project	Converse	Compress
Refuse	Subject	Invalid
Permit	Prospect	Second
Object	Convict	Accent
Conduct	Suspect	Digest
Reject	Extract	Exploit
Present	Abstract	Minute
Increase		

The use of dictionaries should be encouraged.

8 WHAT DO YOU MEAN?   (Levels A, B & C)

This exercise works best if done in small groups (say 5s)

It has been said that there would be no arguments if only people could first agree on the meanings of the words they use.

1 Explain that vague and woolly definitions only confuse others, so the following golden rules must be applied to any explanations that are made: (Write these rules on the board.)

They must be   1 simple and clear
                   2 correctly expressed
                   3 specific to the subject being defined

They must *not* be   1 too general
                     2 too limited
                     3 too joky to be useful

2 Now write on the board the following definitions. Have the class criticise them according to the rules above.

a A clock is an instrument for measuring time.
    (too general – excludes a watch, a chronometer and a sundial)

b Ink is a black liquid used for writing.
    (too limited – excludes other colours)

c A cauliflower is a cabbage with a college education.
    (clever, but perhaps too joky, and not clear)

d A stool is a topless chair.
    (??)

3 Write the following words on the board and have the pupils in their groups write definitions for them.

LEVEL A	LEVEL B	LEVEL C
Diary	Piano	Geologist
Mustard	Argument	Politician

Blindness	Prune	Boys
Snake	Genius	Anatomy
Breadknife	Words	Telephone
Wrist	Hang-over	Barber
Bicycle	Vacuum cleaner	Terrorist
Violin	Pulpit	Cricket
Kangaroo	King	Scissors
Piano	Camera	Martyr
Mat	Helicopter	Bikini
Fashion	Coward	Undertaker
Fog	Girls	Religion
Music	Sinner	Maths
Hairdresser	Tourist	Climate

When the work is complete (or 10 minutes or so from the end of the lesson), ask each group to appoint one representative to sit on a panel of judges.

The panel then hears the sentences read out and allocates points, 3, 2 or 1 according the the quality (precision) of the sentence.

A judge may not vote on sentences from his/her group.

9 KNOW YOUR QUANTITIES (Levels A, B & C)

This activity can be done in pairs or in groups.

The use of dictionaries should be encouraged.

For the weaker groups, the first letter of the word required could be given.

1 Divide the class into working groups.

Explain that in the Wundaworld Safari Park, the pupils will see groups of animals, birds, insects and fish.

Write the following list of such creatures on the board and ask the pupils to find the word (collective noun) for **A GROUP OF** each of them:

e.g. CATTLE → a *herd* of cattle

Allow 5–10 minutes for discussion before checking the results.

sheep (flock)	elephants (herd)	fish (shoal)
bees (swarm/flight)	wolves (pack)	locusts (plague)
lions (pride)	insects (cloud)	chickens (brood)
camels (train)	whales (school)	puppies (litter)
badgers (set)	geese (gaggle)	wild geese in flight (skein)

2 Explain that we sometimes use parts of words from other languages to describe how many things we have:

e.g. *TRI*CYCLE → 3 wheels

*QUAD*RANGLE has (?) sides

Write the following list of words on the board and ask the pupils to explain how many things they have for each of the words. Allow 5–10 minutes discussion before checking the results with the class. A number of interesting connotations will emerge during the discussion between teacher and class.

hexagon (6)	quintet (5)	unity (1)	sextet (6)
triangle (3)	heptagon (7)	septet (7)	pentagon (5)
monocle (1)	dioxide (2)	bicycle (2)	
century (100)	quadruplets (4)	tetragon (4)	

3 Explain that general objects and people are also given special words to describe a number of them. Write the following list on

the board and have the pupils find the word that we use for A NUMBER OF each one.

Allow 10 minutes before checking the results with the class.

drawers (chest)	men's clothes (suit)	bells (peal)
eternal time (eon)	actors (troupe)	eggs (clutch)
grapes (bunch)		tears (flood)
stairs (flight)	pictures (gallery)	beauties (bevy)
tables (nest)	playing cards (pack)	witches (coven)
keys (bunch)	ships (fleet)	thieves (gang)
singers (choir)	scissors (pair)	sailors (crew)
office workers (staff)	angry people (mob)	trees (clump or stand)
people in church (congregation)	mountains (chain/range)	cakes (batch)
arrows (quiver)	furniture (suite)	cutlery (canteen)

If time allows, the pupils could be asked to write some of the more difficult collective nouns in good sentences.

10 EQUALS AND OPPOSITES (Levels A, B & C)

This is a good activity to encourage precise thinking and to expand awareness of how language works.

The activities may be done individually, in pairs, or in small groups.

1   Everything, including our vocabulary, has equals and opposites. Sometimes we use a phrase to explain a contrary idea; sometimes, if we choose our words carefully, we can use just one word e.g. good-bad, high-low.

Such words are known as ANTONYMS.

See how exact an opposite you can find to the following:

LEVEL A	LEVEL B	LEVEL C
open (shut)	superior (inferior)	transparent (opaque)
sweet (sour)	temporary (permanent)	vague (precise)
feeble (strong)	barren (fertile)	conceal (reveal)
broad (narrow)	deep (shallow)	none (all)
hell (heaven)	minimum (maximum)	gaunt (plump)
careful (careless)	victory (defeat)	majority (minority)
gigantic (tiny)	encourage (discourage)	cowardly (heroic)
fresh (stale)	wild (tame)	strict (lax)
proud (humble)	refuse (grant/allow)	overt (covert)
friend (foe)	cramped (spacious)	foreign (native)

2   We can also create opposites by adding a few letters to the front of words. These additions are what are called PREFIXES e.g. known – UNknown. The most common of our prefixes are UN– and IN–, though there are others we can use. Can the class make a list of them?

3   Now ask the class to see if they can create words which mean the *opposite* to those written below by simply adding one or more letters to the front of the words:

LEVEL A	LEVEL B	LEVEL C
do (undo)	regular (irregular)	loyal (disloyal)
human (inhuman)	legal (illegal)	noble (ignoble)
just (unjust)	connect (disconnect)	reverent (irreverent)
obey (disobey)	direct (indirect)	normal (abnormal)
approve (disapprove)	inform (misinform)	audible (inaudible)
correct (incorrect)	relevant (irrelevant)	sense (nonsense)
reliable (unreliable)	similar (dissimilar)	perfect (imperfect)
like (dislike)	proper (improper)	function (malfunction)
septic (antiseptic)	social (antisocial)	count (miscount)
suitable (unsuitable)	sensitise (desensitise)	arm (disarm)

11   KNOW YOUR ADJECTIVES   (Levels B & C)

This is an activity which could be done individually, but it is probably more effective if done in pairs or small groups that allow for quiet discussion.

The use of dictionaries should be encouraged.

1   Divide the class into working pairs or groups.
     Write the following list of places on the board.
     Explain to the pupils that they should find the *ADJECTIVES*
     which come from, or are associated with, these places.
     Allow 10 minutes for discussion before checking on the results
     with the class.

Aberdeen (Aberdonian)	Norway (Norwegian)	Moscow (Muscovite)
Poland (Polish)	Iraq (Iraqi)	Switzerland (Swiss)
Denmark (Danish)	Belgium (Belgian)	Shropshire (Salopian)
Florence (Florentine)	Venice (Venetian)	Wales (Welsh)
Glasgow (Glaswegian)	Eton (Etonian)	Egypt (Egyptian)
Liverpool (Liverpudlian)	Isle of Man (Manx)	Portugal (Portuguese)
Manchester (Mancunian)	Harrow (Harrovian)	Flanders (Flemish)
Oxford (Oxonian)	Naples (Neopolitan)	Yugoslavia (Yugoslav)
Finland (Finnish)	Cornwall (Cornish)	Netherlands (Dutch)
Rome (Roman)	Athens (Athenian)	Cambridge (Cantabrian)

Note: Insist on the correct spelling!

Are there a few local words that can be introduced? e.g.
Liverpudlian – Scouse. Do Mancunians have a less formal
description? Why 'Salopian' for a Shropshire lad?

2   Write the following list of words on the board.
     Explain to the pupils that they should form *ADJECTIVES*
     from the words.
     Again, insist on the correct spelling of the words

Allow 10 minutes for discussion before checking on the results with the class.

cook (cookery)	nonsense (nonsensical)
fame (famous)	climate (climatic)
clarity (clear)	remedy (remedial)
anxiety (anxious)	tactics (tactical)
authenticity (authentic)	suicide (suicidal)
brevity (brief)	omen (ominous)
prophet (prophetic)	joke (jocular)
notoriety (notorious)	diet (dietary)
spectacle (spectacular)	chaos (chaotic)
gas (gaseous)	nucleus (nuclear)

The discussion of these adjectives can lead into all sorts of interesting by-ways.

3 Explain to the pupils that it often happens that the *NAMES of gods or people* (alive or dead, real or imaginary) are used to form adjectives. Write the following list on the board and ask the pupils:

(a) to find the adjectives from the names given;

(b) to say what the adjectives mean.

Allow 5–10 minutes for discussion before checking the results.

Mercury (mercurial) Hercules (herculean) Jove (jovial)

Pasteur (pasteurised) Mars (martial)   Satan (satanic)

Mesmer (mesmerised)   Galvani (galvanised)

Many of the words, e.g. galvanised, will need considerable explanation. In fact, each one has a story – making a good subject for research and writing for homework.

This exercise encourages discussion and constructive pair or group work. It may also be used to give practice in the use of a dictionary. To help the search for answers, the first letter of the correct word may be given.

We know that the animals went into the ark two by two – that is to say, in pairs. However, we often want to refer to larger groups of different animals. Not all creatures move about in *herds* or *flocks*.

Ask the pupils to see if they can find the correct term to describe groups of the following birds or animals, e.g. BUFFALO – a *herd* of buffalo.

LEVEL B (1)	a	of LIONS (pride)
	a	of FISH (shoal)
	a	of HOUNDS (pack/cry)
	a	of LADIES (bevy)
	a	of PORPOISES (school/herd/pod)
	a	of SHEEP (herd/mob/flock)
	a	of SPARROWS (host)
	a	of WOLVES (pack)
	a	of PENGUINS (rookery)
	a	of MONKEYS (troop)
LEVEL B (2)	a	of BEES (swarm)
	a	of CHICKENS (brood/clutch)
	a	of CUBS/PUPS (litter)
	a	of DEER (herd/mob)
	a	of FLIES (cloud)
	a	of GEESE (gaggle)
	a	of BADGERS (cete)
	a	of LOCUSTS (swarm/plague)
	a	of RABBITS (nest)
	a	of SWALLOWS (flight)
LEVEL C (1)	a	of BEARS (sloth)
	a	of DUCKS ON WATER (raft)
	a	of KANGAROOS (mob/troop)
	a	of KITTENS (kindle)
	a	of MONKEYS (troop)
	a	of MULES (barren)
	a	of RACEHORSES (string)

	a	of ROOKS (parliament)
	a	of STARLINGS (murmuration)
	a	of LEOPARDS (leap)
LEVEL C (2)	a	of FOXES (skulk).
	a	of MOLES (labour)
	a	of SPARROWS (host)
	a	of PEACOCKS (muster)
	a	of CATS (clowder)
	a	of MICE (nest)
	a	of COLTS (rag)
	a	of HARES (down)
	a	of COOTS (covert)
	a	of QUAIL (bevy)

Talk it Out

Discussion

13 EQUAL OPPORTUNITIES (Levels B & C)

It is important that we are aware of each other's needs, and of our environment. This exercise (best done in small groups) is aimed at awareness raising.

Set the scene:
Next month, there will be an official visit to your school (town centre) from an important delegation from America. You have been informed that two of the six visitors will be in wheelchairs.

Divide the class into small groups and ask them to:

1   Plan a day's programme for the delegation – arriving at 9.30 a.m. and leaving at 3.30 p.m.
     Discuss (a) what they might like to see;
              (b) how you might be able to ensure access to buildings or display areas so that all the delegation will be able to take part fully in the visits;
              (c) how you might overcome any problems of accessibility.

2   Prepare a report for those in authority as to how you feel your school (or town centre) could be improved for people with mobility difficulties.

3   Share these ideas with other groups.
      Have they thought of anything you have taken for granted or
     overlooked?

4   Consider, if you could make just *one* change to your school (town
     centre) to make it more user-friendly for people in wheelchairs,
     what would it be?

14 RADIO 7   (Levels A, B & C)

This activity should be undertaken in small groups.
      If you have access to a/some portable tape recorder(s) in order to
tape the end results of the group work, it would add an extra element
of 'realism' to the task.

Set the scene
Your school has been invited by BBC radio to provide material for a
three-minute slot about the school, its pupils and its work. This
presentation is to be used as part of an hour-long documentary on
schools and education in different parts of the world and your school
has been chosen as one of three in Britain (ask the pupils why they
might feel that this might be so?).
      The documentary will be broadcast to pupils in the BBC Schools
Programme and on the World Service. It will be aimed at an
international audience of people aged between 9 and 16 years.
      Divide the class into small groups, who should work for about 30
minutes.

1   Ask them to discuss what aspects of the school, its work, the
     teachers and the pupils they feel would be of interest for the
     programme.
          They should list their ideas – what will they put in?
                                       – what will they leave out?
          Remember, that they are going to be talking to people who will
     have never seen their school and who may not even know where
     it is!

2   Instruct each group to write a script for the broadcast – that is, to
     compile material for three minutes' talking time.

Pupils may choose any style they feel is appropriate:
an interview with pupils (and staff?)
a report read by one person?

They may include music/singing if they have those talents in their groups.

The broadcast should be made as interesting as possible. Ask the pupils to suggest how they think this could be achieved. They might consider the following:

- a variety of different people taking part – boys/girls – different nationalities
- a variety of tones of voice to make the presentation sound as interesting as possible
- a variety of material – a human story to illustrate success in classwork, exams, sport, music or drama.

Remind the groups to try and reflect the variety of activities and facilities the school has to offer.

They should also remember that they have only 3 MINUTES OF SPEAKING TIME; that is, 180 seconds!

3   When the scripts have been completed, and those who are taking part in the group's presentations have practised their parts, try recording the programme onto tape for playback to the whole class.

If a tape recorder is not available, do the presentations live to the class.

4   When the presentations have been made to the class, discuss with the other groups what they felt were the best parts of each recording, and why.

15 BALLOON DEBATES   (Levels A, B & C)

Up to 10 famous people are crowded into the basket suspended beneath a hot-air balloon which has a slow leak. The only way to have one survivor of the fated journey is for the others to be thrown out to keep the balloon airborne. The debate has to decide which person in the basket is most worth preserving for the future of mankind.

Preparation for the debate can be done individually, in pairs, or in small groups.

1   Have each person/group choose one famous person, real or fictional, dead or alive.

Get the pupils to work out and note down all the possible arguments in favour of their choices, including defences against points that might be brought up by the opposition.
Work should also be done on how best to present the argument (for example, saving the most important or dramatic point till last) and on deciding which part of the 'case' each pupil will put across. (There is no problem here if the task is done individually. If pairs or groups are used, those not chosen to 'be' the candidate should assume the roles of seconders and present one or two extra arguments supporting the claims of their candidates.)
Allow about 10–15 minutes for this preparation.

2   Have the groups come together for the debate in a semi-formal arrangement. Each speaker/group of speakers should present the case for the chosen candidate to the class as a whole. Voting should be as 'genuine' as possible, and the announcement of the survivor by you, the Chairman, ends the activity.

ALTERNATIVE TOPICS FOR THE DEBATES

1   The best form of transport for the general public is:
car, bicycle, bus, train, roller-skates, horse.

2   The most useful subject to study at school is:
English, Physics, Cooking, Art, Maths, Music.

3   The best spare-time activity is:
football, swimming, cooking, computers, train-spotting, reading.

16 ELECTION TIME (Levels A, B & C)

This is a group activity.
The leader of any country has a difficult job, whether the person is Prime Minister, President, Dictator, King or Queen.

1 Discuss with the pupils the difference between the different titles and offices mentioned above. Try and keep the pupils to the facts, not opinions or prejudices (explain the difference).

2 Divide the class into small groups.
Ask each group to list in order of priority the top 10 attributes that they think a good Prime Minister should have, e.g. honesty, toughness, charm, knowledge, experience, determination, good health.
(Allow about 5 minutes for this.)
Now choose one person from each group in turn to write the group's priorities on the board.

3 When all the lists are on the board, have the pupils discuss the ideas presented, and try to come to some majority decision as to which attributes should be possessed.

4 Now choose a candidate for the office of Prime Minister from each group.
Have the group work out together an election speech which will leave the others in no doubt as to who the best candidate is.

5 Run the election campaign.
Have the candidates present their prepared speeches to the whole class with everything they have got!
Votes could be taken, keeping in mind:

a the quality of the delivery;

b the ideas presented;

c the candidate who swept the voters off their feet! i.e. the power of persuasion;

d the likelihood or possibility of his/her being able to keep the promises made.

17 THE COMPUTER WORLD (Levels B & C)

This activity is in two parts:

PART ONE should be done as a class discussion to guide the
thinking of the pupils;

PART TWO should be done as pair or small group work with one
member of the group or pair writing down their ideas for
reading out to the class at the end of the lesson.

PART ONE

The following suggestions can be used to lead the discussion on
computers and robots.

1   If you had unlimited money, which home computer would you
like to possess, and why?

2   What do you consider the most important functions a home
computer should be able to perform?
(The teacher should write the suggestions on the board.)
Now choose the top 5 functions and list them in order of
importance (the final list should be arrived at by a consensus).

3   What do you think will be the 5 main things that a computer
will be able to do to make life easier in the home of the future?
(The teacher should list these on the board.)

4   Many people think the future home computers will be robots.
Do you agree? Why, or why not?

5   What are the advantages and disadvantages a robot might have
compared with a more conventional computer?

6   Do you think robots could ever become the enemy of human
beings? What might happen? How could we avoid this?

PART TWO

Divide the pupils into groups to discuss and work on the following
situations. (One member of the group should write down an agreed
version to read to the class at the end of the lesson.)
You may wish to have some groups discussing option 'A' and

others discussing option 'B'. It is also possible for all groups to work on both 'A' and 'B'.

OPTION A

A DAY IN THE LIFE OF MARVIN THE HOMEMAKER
Imagine you are Marvin, the robot.
An important magazine has asked you to send it a tape in which you discuss a typical 24-hour day, describing in detail your life in the home. Think of what will interest people; leave out obvious things like 'I get out of bed' and introduce your personal feelings about the events.

OPTION B

A DAY IN THE LIFE OF HAROLD THE SCHOOLMATE
Imagine you are Harold, the robot.
An important magazine has asked you to send it a tape describing a typical day at school.
There will be several types of lesson, and several teachers.
Remember to express your FEELINGS about what you enjoy, hate or endure.

---

18 THE IDEAL HOME (Levels A, B & C)

This is an activity for group discussion on a domestic and very interesting subject.

1   Divide the class into small discussion groups and explain that they are going to try and come to an agreement on what they think would be the IDEAL HOME for the average Mr & Mrs BRITAIN.

2   Explain that the discussion will be done under various headings, which you will write on the board, as below.
Allow about 10 minutes discussion, and then bring the groups together to pool their ideas and try to come to an agreement about this 'architect-designed' home of their imagination.

HEADINGS

a   *TYPE:* wooden, glass, plastic, brick etc.
       a cottage, in a block of flats, a bungalow etc.
       modern, 20, 50, 100, 200 years old etc.

b   *SITUATION:* on a main road, by a river, on the 23rd
       floor of a city block etc.

c   *INSIDE OF HOUSE:* how many rooms, which rooms etc.

d   *GARDEN:* concrete yard, pool, lawn, trees, shrubs etc.

e   *STYLE OF FURNITURE:* modern, antique etc.

3   Now explain to the groups that you will write on the board a list of appliances and devices and that Mr & Mrs Britain are permitted to have only 10 of them. Which 10 should these be? Have the groups list their choices in order of importance. (Allow 5 minutes discussion, and then bring the groups together to pool their ideas and try to come to a consensus.)

APPLIANCES AND DEVICES (they already have a cooker and refrigerator)

washing machine	video	liquidiser	television
microwave oven	floor polisher	stereo	hair dryer
spin dryer	stainless steel sink	dishwasher	deep freeze
vacuum cleaner	food mixer	telephone	home computer

4   *WHAT ABOUT COLOURS?*

Write the following lists of colours and criteria on the board and ask the groups to list the colours 1–6 according to each criterion. (Allow 6–8 minutes for discussion, and then pool the groups' ideas and discuss the decisions made.)

COLOURS: red violet green brown white blue

CRITERIA: restful cheerful cool warm useful stimulating

Have the pupils decide on the ideal colour scheme for Mr & Mrs Britain's home. (They may use colours not already mentioned in previous exercises.)

FOLLOW-UP

A   Ask the pupils to describe in a few sentences how they would spend a big sum of money they have just won, on making their *own* home more comfortable and beautiful.

B   The number of topics that can arise is obviously endless. For example, why is the cost of a 'personalised' house so high? What types of houses do people normally have to be content with, and what faults do they find?

VARIATION (Levels B & C)

People of different ages and types will have different ideas on what makes the ideal home. Choose one of the biographies below and have the groups discuss the various topics, 2–4, according to the specific information they now have on Mr & Mrs Britain.

i	Mr & Mrs Britain	retired couple, sociable, 2 grandchildren. Mrs Britain likes sewing, gardening, goldfish, painting. Mr Britain likes sport, woodwork, television.
ii	Mr & Mrs Britain	both are teachers in their 40's, 2 teenage children. Like entertaining at home. Mrs Britain is writing a book; Mr Britain is a TV fanatic.
iii	Mr & Mrs Britain	both are in their 20's, married 18 months ago, have a baby boy. Mrs Britain likes cooking, does typing at home. Mr Britain likes photography (does his own developing), and reading.

This activity is in 3 parts, and is best done as follows:

1   in groups of 4;

2   in pairs;

3   individually.

PART ONE

Divide the class into groups of about 4.
Make sure there is *an even number* of groups, even though some
may not be 4s.
Label one half of the groups 'A' and the balancing half 'B'.
Have the groups discuss the following situations for 10–15
minutes.

GROUPS 'A'
It is the year 2086

Explain to the pupils that each group 'A' is a person who is
famous throughout the world. The person may be a pop star, a
scientist, a musician, a politician – any FAMOUS person at all.
In the groups, they should choose who the person is going to be,
and create a biography for him/her.
They should include such things as

        – date and place of birth
        – early life
        – when and why he/she became famous
        – likes and dislikes
        – thoughts on world affairs
        – hopes for the future
        – a 'secret life' story

Each member of the group should write down the details agreed
on as each member will act the part of the famous person in
Part 2.

GROUPS 'B'

It is the same year – 2086

Explain to the pupils that each group in the 'B' half is a group of reporters for the local newspaper, 'The Echo'. They are being sent to interview a famous person who is visiting their town for one day.

In the groups they should work out the questions they think they should ask to get all the information they can about the visiting personality: e.g. In your home or school, Mr Racine, was there any one particular person who helped you towards success?

PART TWO

When both sets of groups are ready with their questions and information, pupils in groups 'A' should pair off with pupils in groups 'B' to conduct the interview. This should last about 5 minutes. Remind the interviewers that it is wise to start with easy, pleasant questions in order to put the interviewee at ease.

PART THREE

Once information has been gained, the pupils should return to their seats to write up their findings. Pupils from groups 'A' should write out *'a day in the life of'* the personality they represent, to be printed in 'The Echo's' Sunday edition.

Pupils from groups 'B' should write a scoop article for 'The Echo' on the visiting personality – including the headline, e.g.

FAMOUS AUTHOR GETS HIS IDEAS FROM DREAMS

The work can be displayed for all to enjoy.

This activity is best done in small groups.

Explain to the class that one of the big decisions that the pupils will have to make in life is what they will do with themselves after their schooling is over.

This activity will look at how to decide what job to choose.

1   Divide the class into small discussion groups.
Write the following list of jobs on the board.
Ask the pupils to see if they can write a brief but accurate description of three of them, which would include what the person does in the job.

a disc-jockey	a secretary
a solicitor	a radio operator on a ship
a model	a policeman
an air hostess	a nurse
an estate agent	a shop assistant
an airline pilot	an engineer

Allow 10 minutes for discussion, then have each group in turn give you one definition. See if other groups agree, and encourage them to improve on the explanation.

2   Now explain to the groups that certain jobs are best done when the workers have certain qualities or personalities. Ask the pupils to give you as many *good points* in a person's character as possible. Write these on the board as they are fired at you. You might begin with CHARM, HONESTY, ACCURACY, PATIENCE. ... (use only *half* the board; label this *LIST A*).

3   Now ask each group to give you 2–3 jobs people do – for example BUS DRIVER, ENGINEER, POTTER. Write these on the board and label them *LIST B*.

4   Have the groups discuss the lists to find for each of the jobs
     presented in List B, the *5 most important qualities* from List A that
     are needed to be a successful worker in each of the jobs. The
     groups should list these qualities 1–5 in order of importance to
     the job.
     Allow about 15 minutes for the discussion.

5   Finally, have the pupils report their findings back to the class as
     a whole.
     Discuss these and try to come to a consensus.

6   If time allows, try to stimulate a discussion on the nature of
     UNUSUAL JOBS, and how people get into them e.g.

     an inspector of sewers

     a zoo keeper/assistant

     a vivisectionist ... plenty of argument will follow!

     a thatcher

     a radiographer

     a restorer of antique furniture

     a ceramic artist

     a saggar-maker's bottom knocker (!)

     a steeplejack

     a diver

Solve this One

Problem solving

---

21 SURVIVAL   (Levels A, B & C)

---

1   Divide the class into discussion groups, of not more than 5. (A small enough group to discuss quietly round a small table.)

2   Set the scene as follows:
Imagine you have been a passenger in an aeroplane which has crashed into a mountain 2000 metres high. You have escaped with only shock and minor burns. There is snow all around you. From amongst the wreckage you find the following items. Number them in order of necessity for your survival (1 is the most important, 15 the least important).

    a box of matches

    signal flares

    first aid kit

    parachute

    three wooden cases of dehydrated milk

    25 litres of fresh water

    a life-jacket

50 metres of nylon rope

a map of the mountain area

a bottle of whisky

an inflatable raft

a pair of sunglasses

3 woollen blankets

a battery-run transistor radio

an army-knife

(This list can be written on the board)

3   Give the groups 20 minutes for discussion.

4   When they have decided on their orders of priority, bring the
     groups back together for the feedback session. The aim is to try
     and come to a general definitive solution after comparing the
     results of the groups and discussing the differences. The
     discussion will be tidier if a speaker for each group is elected to
     lead for the group. The others do not have to remain silent; they
     will want to reinforce their representative's points from time to
     time. As there is no one correct answer, any sensible solution
     should be accepted so long as all possible uses of the individual
     items have been understood, e.g. the parachute could be used to
     build a shelter.

     The following might also be considered by the different levels.

LEVEL A

You have gone fishing and your boat has drifted out to sea out
of sight of land. You have:

a box of matches

oars

an oil-lamp with oil

binoculars

a fisherman's knife

a lifebelt

string

a bottle of water

a small sail, and mast

a compass

fish-hooks and fishing rod

a book

a pencil

some chocolate

a bucket

LEVEL C

You are with an expedition exploring at the North Pole. You have become separated from your companions by a snowstorm. You have:

a small sledge

a 5 litre can of water (frozen)

a tin of sardines

a first aid kit

a box of matches

a pair of sunglasses

a Husky to pull the sledge

a magnetic compass

a camper's stove and gas

30 metres of rope

2 flares

a bottle of brandy

a sleeping-bag

a stretcher

a hunting-knife

a car battery

a radio receiver

The lists can either be dictated, or displayed on the board.

22 PICTOGRAMS (Levels A, B & C)

This is an activity for individuals, pairs or small groups. The pupils will enjoy pitting their wits against others', and they will be asked to bring into play their powers of encoding and decoding.

At Level A the messsage may be short and simple.

At Level C there may be more complex words to deal with and longer messages may be expected.

Essentially, the activity involves the displaying of a message in picture form as follows.

1   Each picture may represent a whole word

e.g.   (ewe) = you

or a part of a word

e.g.  8   Oh Oh   (pot eight Ohs) = potatoes

2   New letters may be substituted for those not required

e.g.   b̷   L   (bike − b = ike + L) = like

3   Letters at the beginning and end of a word may be removed

e.g.   (cat − c) = at   c̷

An enjoyable competitive element may be introduced by asking the pupils to write messages for other groups to decode and answer.

For all levels, correct spelling of the decoded message is essential.

To provide inspiration the following could be used as examples:

23 HETTY HIGGINS (Levels A, B & C)

This game aims to have fun with spelling, and to test the pupils' powers of deduction.

As the name of the game suggests, words containing *double letters* are the ones to be considered (though there are other categories of words that can be used as well).

Have the pupils seated in a rough circle so that they can take turns to speak in an orderly manner. Include yourself in this circle. Set the scene as follows:

We are going to discuss a very strange girl called Hetty Higgins. She is strange because she likes an odd combination of things, and sometimes seems to contradict herself when she says she likes one thing but doesn't like another. For example, she likes *sweets* but doesn't like *chocolate*, and she likes *looking* at TV but doesn't like *watching* it. I want each of you to try and work out what kinds of things Hetty likes by a process of elimination. Each of you in turn will say, "Hetty Higgins likes … x … but doesn't like … y …" If you have chosen the correct likes and dislikes I will say, "yes." If you haven't made the right choice, I will say, "no." You may choose anything you like. At first you will have to guess what Hetty likes but, if you really think about the things which I say are correct, you should soon know the types of things to say.

When you think you have found the clue to Hetty's strange habits, DON'T tell anyone what the answer is. Simply continue, when it is your turn, to say the correct things. Let's see how good your detective powers are.

Begin the game yourself:

Hetty Higgins likes *cabbage* but doesn't like *tomatoes*. The pupil next to you in a clockwise direction should then try, and so on round the class. If a pupil is not successful, don't pause or have a post mortem – continue with the next pupil so that the words that are required are deduced by the players from the examples given in the correct statements.

Try and keep the pace moving – don't allow more than a couple of seconds for thinking.

The game has no set time limit – it can continue till the last pupil has found the key.

OTHER POSSIBILITIES

1   HETTY HIGGINS likes words with 2 syllables only.

e.g. Hetty Higgins likes *papers* but not *magazines*.
Hetty Higgins likes to *begin* things, but not to *end* them.

2   STEPHEN STALKER (a cousin of Hetty) likes words with silent letters including: final silent R; silent K as in knee; and foreign words: restaurant; ballet.

e.g. Stephen Stalker likes to chee*r*, but not to shout.
Stephen Stalker likes *k*nowledge, but not information.
Stephen Stalker likes ha*l*ves, but not seconds.

This activity can be done individually, in pairs, or in small groups.

a   Write the following *logic wheels* and *magic squares* on the board.

b   Have the pupils copy them down and use their detective powers to find the missing letters.

I

2

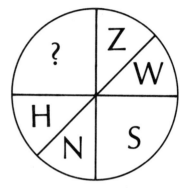

3

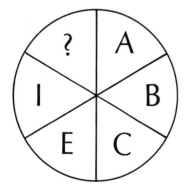

4

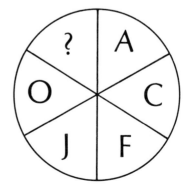

5

6

```
Y  V   X  W
O  I   M  K
T  K   Q  ?
```

```
H  M   I  L
U  Z   V  Y
B  ?   C  F
```

ANSWERS 1 C; 2 A; 3 Q; 4 W; 5 Q; 6 U; 7 N; 8 G

FOLLOW-UP ACTIVITIES

c   Have the pupils create their own logic wheels and magic squares.

d   Take *logic wheel 1 or magic square 4* and have the pupils see how many words can be made from the letters there.

25   THE PUBLICITY CAMPAIGN
(Levels A, B & C)

Divide the class into groups of four pupils, then set the scene as follows:

Your local council has a problem. It would like to spend money on an advertising campaign to promote your area as a tourist attraction, but it is not sure to which agency to give the job. Therefore, a competition has been announced to find out which agency can offer the best advertisements.

Two things must be submitted:

1   a pamphlet;

2   a script for a short TV advertisement.

Each group is an agency in the competition.

1   Ask the pupils to tell you what they think makes up a good advertisement.
    Write up on the board the suggestions they give you.
    The following 6 points will help to get the discussion going.

    1   It catches the eye and/or attention.

    2   It holds the attention.

    3   It is not too long.

    4   It is easy to remember.

    5   It praises the good qualities/discourages the bad elements.

    6   It encourages the listener/reader/viewer to do something about it.

2   Have the pupils plan their campaigns carefully. They should discuss in their groups what should be in the pamphlet and in the TV programme. For example, should the latter be an interview, or a jingle to go with a series of pictures of the area? They should also decide on a division of labour – perhaps 2 to do the pamphlet and 2 to do the TV programme.

3   Have the pupils prepare their exhibits to be displayed at the end of the lesson.
    As you are among the groups while they are working, you are bound to discover one or two outstanding 'productions' of the TV interview. Try to leave time at the end of the lesson for at least 2 of these to be performed to the class.

OTHER SUGGESTIONS

End pollution of the countryside

The police are your friends

Every family should own a computer

School lunches should be free

Your new pedestrian precinct

Don't go home with a stranger

Your local theatre needs publicity

This activity is best done in pairs, or in small groups.

Explain that a group of people of widely different types is to be arranged in a way that will create the least friction among them. It is therefore important to take into account each person's different limitations, relationships and individual quirks.

There is not necessarily *one* correct answer. Any sensible and defensible layout can be accepted. A compromise is usually the best solution.

1   Divide the pupils into pairs or small discussion groups and ask them to appoint a group leader.

2   Explain the problem as follows:

You are the Social Committee for your town/area and have organised a day's outing – a mystery coach trip – to be sponsored by a local firm.
Enough people have said they will come to enable you to fill a minibus but, on examination of the passenger list, you find you have a very varied group of people. From the biographies I shall put on the board, sort out the seating plan which you think will ensure that everyone has a good chance of enjoying the day.
The bus seats 14 people:

5 at the back;
2 rows of 2 on each side;
1 near the driver.

Allow about 20 minutes for the discussion. Ask each group to draw a plan of the seating and to put in the names.

3   In the *FEEDBACK SESSION* the group leaders should write their proposals on the board for comparison, discussion and possible adjustment in the light of the other groups' ideas.
It is helpful if you guide the groups to remind them of all the implications of the problem. You can also offer other combinations for the different groups to think about. They must also explain – and argue about – the reasons for their allocation of seats.

BIOGRAPHIES (to be written on the board for use during the discussion)

Sue aged 25   Well-educated, sociable, ambitious, hard-working.

Paul aged 24   Aggressive, unemployed, in and out of prison.

John aged 18   Unemployed and can't find work, sociable, lively.

Pam aged 20   Hippy, talkative, not well-educated, a drifter.

Bill aged 40   Successful businessman, loud, boasts about money and properties.

Jackie aged 50   Hard-of-hearing, talkative but repeats herself, talks about her family and the war.

Mark aged 16   Shy, quiet, polite.

Jill aged 17   Noisy, overpowering personality.

Jim aged 34   Family died in a car accident, withdrawn, suicidal.

Siz aged 19   Punk, dyed hair, sociable, talks loudly about nothing.

Katy aged 47   A matron in the local hospital, friendly but stern and bossy.

Henry aged 27   Social worker, lively, cheerful, chatty, likes sorting out people's problems.

Lisa aged 40   Secretary, reserved, prim and proper.

James aged 41   Teacher of English, bossy, know-all, talkative.

There is one separate single seat. How many students would allocate that seat to the loner, Jim?

ALTERNATIVE

You have organised a mystery tour by bus for your class. Arrange the seating plan so that everyone will enjoy the trip.

27 THE NOBEL PRIZE WINNERS
(Levels A, B & C)

PART ONE of this activity should be done in small discussion groups.
PART TWO should be done by individuals.

PART ONE

Divide the pupils into groups and explain that this year is a special anniversary year for Nobel Prizes. The groups represent the Prize Committee whose job is to choose the winners. This year, it has been decided to award a special prize to the candidate thought to have done the most for other people. The committee must choose from the following list of finalists (which should be written on the board).

> Princess Anne, Pope John Paul II, Bob Geldof, Mother Theresa, Mahatma Gandhi, Henri Dunant (founder of the Red Cross), Florence Nightingale, The United Nations Organisation, Louis Braille

First spend a few minutes making sure that the students understand who or what these people and organisations are, then have the pupils discuss which candidate should receive the Anniversary Medal.
If a candidate is now dead, the medal will be presented to the Mayor of the candidate's home town.
When their choices have been made, the groups should prepare short speeches which will be read out at the presentation ceremony, explaining to the world why their successful finalists were chosen.
Allow 10–15 minutes for discussion and preparation of the speeches – they should be *written*, at least in note form, but preferably in full text.
Bring the groups together to discuss the choices and present the speeches.

PART TWO

Now, have each pupil imagine he/she is the chairperson of the committee and thus can award his/her own 'Chairperson's Nobel

Prize'. Each pupil should, therefore, choose his/her hero or heroine – anyone from the beginning of time to the present day – who should be recognised as the greatest person who has ever lived on earth.

Have *each pupil* prepare a short speech which could be read out at the presentation ceremony. The award will be presented to the Mayor of the home town of the person chosen.

Allow about 10 minutes for this section, and finish the lesson with one or two selections from the individual choices and speeches.

AN ALTERNATIVE CRITERION FOR PART ONE

This year it has been decided to award a special prize for the greatest contribution to *SCIENCE*. The committee must choose from the following list of finalists, which you should write on the board:

Clive Sinclair, Alexander Bell, Marie Curie, Thomas Edison, John Logie Baird, Louis Pasteur, Ernest Rutherford

Again, it will first be necessary to make sure that the pupils know exactly for what each person is famous (Chambers Biographical Dictionary – almost certainly in the school library – is the ideal reference book here).

Everyone's a Writer

Poetry and short story writing

28   THE KITE   (Levels A, B & C)

Writing accurately demands precision of thought and discipline in putting ideas down on paper. (But you may need to explain that in simpler terms.)

KITE-FLYING is a form of writing which encourages such discipline. It is best done individually by members of the class.

The exercise involves the pupils counting the number of syllables in each line they write and building up a structure with the following pattern

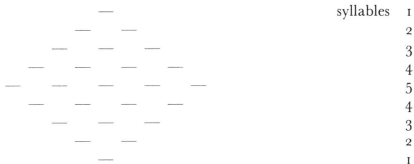

	syllables 1
	2
	3
	4
	5
	4
	3
	2
	1

The number of syllables per line starts with one and increases progressively to 5. It then decreases again to one. The 5-syllable line may contain one word of 5 syllables, 5 words of one syllable, or any other combination adding up to 5.

As an introduction to the exercise, give the pupils a topic such as *SUNRISE* and ask them to give you all the words that they associate with the topic – colours, sights, sounds, movement. Write these on the board. Do not spend more than 3 or 4 minutes doing this.

Then, together with the pupils, fly your kites. Concentrate on one aspect only of a sunrise.

e.g.

> one
>
> ball of
>
> pulsating
>
> vibrant orange
>
> balances on the
>
> grey tightrope that
>
> holds apart
>
> sea and
>
> sky

Now, ask the pupils to choose their own subjects.

Get them to write down their own lists of words associated with the ideas and then encourage them to fly their own kites.

For those who have difficulty choosing a topic, the following suggestions might help.

The cat	e.g.	My	1
Waterfall		Persian	2
The Storm		green-eyed Tom	3
The Old Man		meticulous	4
Night		in his cleanliness	5
		sits washing to	4
		perfection	3
		pale grey	2
		paws	1

They will find, after the first attempt, that it is not difficult at all.

This exercise is best done individually.

The haiku is a traditional form of Japanese verse which introduces the concept of *rhythm* in words. It encourages economy of statement, and a concentration on one aspect of the topic chosen. Pupils of all ages and abilities enjoy the challenge of precision of thought that is required.

It is composed of 3 short lines of 5, 7 and 5 syllables respectively, a total of 17 syllables overall.

. . . . 5 syllables

. . . . 7 syllables

. . . . 5 syllables

As an introduction, you might like to work through an example with the class. In this way the process of 'polishing' to find just the right words and rhythms can be demonstrated, e.g.

THE TREE

Living umbrella,

Open against the downpour

Protecting the earth.

Now encourage the pupils to choose their own subjects. For those who find it hard to start, the following suggestions could be given.

School	Christmas
War	Dreams
A Rose	Fear
Goldfish	The Tortoise
Computers	A Frog

This is a class activity which could later be repeated in pairs or small groups.

If words are carefully combined, powerful moods can be created, and pictures painted in the mind.

As a class exercise, under your guidance, paint a picture by playing with the rhythms and images inherent in words, and working for powerful effects. This is not difficult as long as a brisk working pace is maintained.

1   Ask 3 or 4 pupils at random to give you *a noun*.
    Write the suggestions quickly on the board as they are given to you.

2   Ask the class to choose the one suggestion which looks the most interesting. Rub out the others and rewrite the chosen noun, in title form, at the top of the board.

3   *Now have a brainstorming session.*
    Ask the pupils to fire at you any words and short phrases they can think of which are connected with the chosen topic. Write these on the board, leaving about ⅓ of the board free for the final stage. Fill the space with suggestions. You will have to use a veto on ideas which cannot be depended on as having connections with the topic.

4   With the pupils' help, select the words which fit together in a natural or exciting way and thus which can be used to 'paint a picture' of your topic.
    Write them up in verse form, working for rhythm, flow of words, and picturesque ideas.

For Example: CAT

violent	twitching	night huntress	midnight prowler
playful	darting	amber-eyed	chases
purring	melting into darkness	whiskers	rushing out
sleeper	watchman	soft	undercover
		murderess	winsome

Amber-eyed huntress
Long-whiskered and soft,
Melting into darkness
On the midnight watch;
Darting out from cover
In the rush of violent chase,
Then winsome and purring,
The twitching murderess sleeps.

5   Divide the pupils into pairs or small groups. Have them repeat
     the process on their own.
     Display the finished work for all to share. There will be some
     surprisingly good results.

31 A SOLDIER'S TALE (Level C only)

This is an exercise in guided writing. The pupils will work
individually and will need writing materials.

You will read the pupils the instructions set out below which they
must follow *exactly*. A reasonable time for writing should be allowed
between each step. Each set of instructions will need to be repeated at
least twice.

As a result of the exercise, each pupil will have an original piece of
writing on the theme of DULCE ET DECORUM EST by
Wilfred Owen. (You will have to translate later. DULCE ET
DECORUM EST PRO PATRIA MORI – It is sweet and
seemly to die for one's country.)

The poem is reproduced at the end for reading to the class, and
possibly for discussion by the pupils should time permit. The pupils
might consider such things as:

a   the choices of titles for the poem, and their own
     contributions;

b   a comparison of their adjectives and descriptive phrases with
     those of Owen;

c   whether or not they consider the poem would have had
     more impact if it had been written as a story.

THE EXERCISE

We are going to build up a picture in writing according to some instructions I shall give you.

Listen carefully to the scenes I describe, and then write down what you would like to say about them in the number of lines I give you. Sometimes you will need to write only 1 line, sometimes 3 or 4.

1   Imagine you and your comrades are a group of soldiers on a muddy battlefield. You have been fighting for many months, and are so exhausted you can't stand straight. You are all sick with chest complaints, and cough as you move around in the mud.
In *2 lines* describe the group of soldiers. Remember, you are one of the men.

2.   You are trying to march away from the front line, back to safety and some rest. You leave the bursting shells and flares of the battle behind you.
Describe this in *2 lines*.

3   You describe the men more exactly now.
They appear too tired to think or to see where they are marching. Many have lost their boots, and have cuts on their feet. It is painful to walk. All of them are so very tired that they move like drunken men and don't even hear the sound of the gas-shells which begin to fall behind them.
Use *4 lines* for your description.

4   *EMERGENCY!*
You suddenly realise that you are surrounded by *poisonous gas*. Shout a warning to the others in the group.
Use *1 line* only.

5   Even though you are all exhausted, you use all the speed you can muster to put on the awkward gas masks you carry in your kits. Most of you are successful, but one man is too slow and staggers about, crying out as the gas gets into his lungs.
Describe the scene in *3 lines*.

6   The gas is thick now, a greenish pea-soup colour. It is difficult to

see your comrades through these ghastly clouds.
In *2 lines* describe the scene.

7   You will never forget seeing your comrade come rushing towards you through the gas. You feel totally helpless in the situation as the gas gets into his lungs and he coughs horribly. You know he is going to die.
Describe this in *2 lines*.

8   You are so disgusted by what you see and hear that you now try to involve your readers in your experience. You ask your readers directly to imagine what they would feel like to have to walk behind the wagon carrying the victim and to watch the man writhing and dying in agony.
Use *4 lines* to do this. Include a brief description of what the dying man looks like.

9   In *4 lines* ask the readers to imagine what it would be like to have to listen to the dying man as the movement of the wagon across the uneven ground forces the blood up from his lungs, which are now being turned into blood and mucus by the gas.

10   In your last *4 lines* you want to tell the readers that if they had experienced what you have described, they wouldn't wish to say ever again that it is *glorious* to die for your country.
Say this in any way you feel.

11   Give a title to what you have written.

12   Now read the poem slowly to the class.

Dulce et Decorum Est

Bent double, like old beggars under sacks,
Knock-kneed, coughing like hags, we cursed through sludge,
Till on the haunting flares we turned our backs,
And towards our distant rest began to trudge.
Men marched asleep. Many had lost their boots,
But limped on, blood-shod. All went lame, all blind;
Drunk with fatigue; deaf even to the hoots
Of gas-shells dropping softly behind.

Gas! Gas! Quick, boys! – An ecstasy of fumbling,
Fitting the clumsy helmets just in time,
But someone still was yelling out and stumbling
And floundering like a man in fire or lime. –
Dim through the misty panes and thick green light,
As under a green sea, I saw him drowning.

In all my dreams before my helpless sight
He plunges at me, guttering, choking, drowning.

If in some smothering dreams, you too could pace
Behind the wagon that we flung him in,
And watch the white eyes writhing in his face,
His hanging face, like a devil's sick of sin;
If you could hear, at every jolt, the blood
Come gargling from the froth-corrupted lungs,
Bitter as the cud
Of vile, incurable sores on innocent tongues, –
My friend, you would not tell with such high zest
To children ardent for some desperate glory,
The old Lie: Dulce et decorum est
Pro patria mori.

32 THE INCREDIBLE JOURNEY
(Levels A, B & C)

For this exercise, the pupils can work individually, in pairs, or in small groups of up to 4.

The activity involves using a series of incongruous elements to write a short story about a journey. *All* the elements that are given should be included in the story in the order and form in which they are presented.

On the board, write out the whole set of elements for the class as a whole. If everyone is working on the same set of stimuli, the different results will be a source of entertainment when the stories are read to the other members of the class at the end of the lesson.

The exercise can be lengthened by the addition of an extra word just when the pupils think they have completed the task.

The following are examples of sets of incongruous elements that could be used.

LEVEL A

1   tiger, television, joyful, tulip field, dance, lemonade

2   the Prime Minister, motorway, key, banana, laugh, shakily, "where am I?"

3   actress, aunt, nose, alligator, motionless, paddle, as fast as possible

Example No. 1

> Now you may think it very strange that a young *tiger* should have a *television* set; but the reason is that he never knew he was a tiger. When he was very young indeed, in fact just after he was born, he was found in the long grass by a man who was hunting. So the first living thing the tiger ever saw was this man; this made the young tiger think he too was a human being. He was taken to a house next to a huge *tulip field* and lived with the family. When they watched TV he watched TV. If they could *dance* he could dance – just like any human, only better. When they drank *lemonade*, he drank lemonade. Not that he liked it much, but if they did it he had to do it too. In fact it was a very *joyful* life . . . until the tiger began to grow up. Then he felt quite different . '. . and you can imagine what happened next.

There is a deliberate error in the construction of that 'story'. In what way does it not keep to the rules given?

LEVEL B

1   electronic, skate, greasy, explosively, Napoleon, nail varnish, rhinoceros

2　　microbe, jungle, telephone, snowflake, religiously, potato

3　　elephant, matchbox, vegetarian, double bass, ventriloquist, bride

Example No. 3

Of course it's very difficult to imagine why an *elephant* and a *matchbox* should come into the same story, but they did. Actually, the animal ate the matchbox – he liked wooden things to eat anyway, being a *vegetarian* (I mean, who has ever seen an elephant eating meat?), and actually it was the musician playing the *double bass* who had thrown it to him during a break in the music. Music, you ask? Why music at the zoo? Well, it was a strange day; never anything like it before. A party of people came with this orchestra, all beautifully dressed, especially the ladies. One was all in white, with a veil. The elephant found it very strange, especially when he heard the lady chattering like a monkey. The wedding party was led by a *ventriloquist*, you see, and he thought it funny to get the *bride* to make these zoo noises, even though he was the bridegroom. The elephant was not amused.

LEVEL C

1　　fashion model, Garden of Eden, fossil, congratulate, crocodile, Neil Armstrong, "how are you?"

2　　needle-like, atmosphere, obstruction, inner city, daisy, silicon chip, Siberia, "but it's not cricket"

3　　detective, moon crater, Cleopatra, shark, chocolate cake, gloves, "let's dance"

Example No. 2

Sarah felt as soon as she entered the room a sharp, almost *needle-like* sensation of pain; not a physical pain but an intense and sudden sensation of dislike. Eyes upon her showed distaste. The *atmosphere* was hateful. Here, at once she knew, she would find nothing but *obstruction* to the plans she hoped to explain. That was what *inner city* life did to people; made them distrustful and hateful. People brought up among blocks of concrete had never known grass, or streams, or noted the beauty of a *daisy*, or the delight of a nightingale's song. People spent their days talking about stocks and shares and the *silicon chip*, and growled about the Russian menace, the KGB and the hell of prison in *Siberia*. And if someone did something mean they muttered, "Oh, *but it's not cricket*, old boy!" as though meanness, dishonesty and the disasters of politics were just a game.

Sarah knew without saying a word that they would never really listen. She turned on her heel and abruptly left.

33   DESCRIBING PEOPLE   (Levels A, B & C)

It is very easy to write descriptions of people which are rather ordinary and easily forgettable. It is just as easy to write a pen portrait that brings a person alive and remains memorable for a long time after the words have been read. This exercise is aimed at helping pupils to understand the ingredients that are required to build up descriptions of people who have lives and personalities of their own.

The session should start with a class exercise and then move to pair and/or individual work.

1   Describing people involves writing about what they look like from the *outside* AND what they are like on the *inside*.

With the whole class, as a board exercise, draw up two questionnaires:

(a)   to find out information about what someone might LOOK LIKE;

(b)   to find out what they are like INSIDE.

You might cover such things as:

QUESTIONNAIRE (a)
1   Eye/hair/skin colour
2   Height
3   Size – slim, large, small
4   Something different or special or striking about the way the person looks

5   Why one might remember the person
6   How many friends the person has; whether or not there is a
     'best friend'

QUESTIONNAIRE (b)
1   Things the person is good at
2   Confidence, or lack of it
3   Temper – good or bad
4   Patience
5   Things the person likes or dislikes
6   Special things, like the way the person laughs or walks
7   What kind of animal or flower the person would like to be.
     (What could his/her choice tell you about the person?)

2   Now explain that simply writing a list of facts is not really going
     to bring the person alive. We need to try and make it seem as
     though he or she could walk off the page. We need to find special
     ways of describing people.
        Still with the whole class, compare the following descriptions
     (you may wish to write these up on the board).

     1   (a) My Uncle John is a fat man with big hands
          (b) My Uncle John has fingers like sausages

     2   (a) She was tall, had lots of curly red hair and brown eyes
          (b) She was a tall girl with a mop of red hair in tight curls,
              and large eyes that glowed warmly when she smiled.

     3   (a) She had light-blue eyes
          (b) Her eyes were blue, and reminded me of the sky at dawn

     Now see what descriptions the class can give you to characterise
     the following:

     1   A man with a large, pointed nose
     2   A shy person who never says much
     3   A person who can't stop making funny remarks
     4   Someone with a lovely smile or unusual laugh
     5   A tall, thin person

3   You can choose here how you want to develop this exercise to
     practise written descriptions – either (a) individually, or (b) in pairs.

(a) Individual work

Instruct the pupils to draw up their own family trees. (You may need to draw one of your own quickly on the board to give them a model.)

Ask them to choose one person from their family and make a list of all they know about him/her, following the guidelines set out in the two questionnaires.

The pupils should then write a paragraph describing their chosen relatives in as lively a way as possible.

(b) Pair-work

Divide the class into pairs. Allow seven minutes or so for each pupil to find out and write down information about his/her partner.

Each pupil should then write a paragraph about his/her partner, using the information gained from the interview session.

Pupils should be encouraged to share their final versions with their partners and/or the class.

34 UNLIKELY ORIGINS (Levels A, B & C)

This is an activity for individual work.

Charles Lamb, a writer who lived from 1775 to 1834, once tried to explain in a humorous way the origins of roast pork in the following story. Listen while I read it.

1 Read aloud the story:

How we got Roast Pork

Mankind, says a Chinese manuscript, for the first seventy thousand ages ate their meat raw. The art of roasting, was accidentally discovered in the following manner. The swine-herd, Ho-ti, having gone out into the woods one morning, as his manner was, to collect food for his hogs, left his cottage in the care of his eldest son Bo-bo, a great lubberly boy, who being fond of playing with fire, as children of his age commonly are, let some sparks escape into a bundle of straw, which kindling quickly, spread the conflagration over every part of their poor mansion, till it was reduced to ashes. Together with the cottage, what was of much more importance, a fine litter of new-farrowed pigs, no less than nine in number, perished. China pigs have been thought a luxury all over the East from the remotest periods that we read of. Bo-bo was in the utmost consternation, as you may think, not so much for the sake of the tenement, which his father and he could easily build up again with a few dry branches, and the labour of an hour or two, at any time, as for the loss of the pigs. While he was thinking what he should say to his father, and wringing his hands over the smoking remnants of one of those untimely sufferers, an odour assailed his nostrils, unlike any scent which he had before experienced. What could it proceed from? – not from the burnt cottage – he had smelt that smell before – indeed this was by no means the first accident of the kind which had occurred through the negligence of this unlucky young fire-brand. Much less did it resemble that of any known herb, weed, or flower. He knew not what to think. He next stooped down to feel the pig, if there were any signs of life in it. He burnt his fingers, and to cool them he applied them in his booby fashion to his mouth. Some of the crumbs of the scorched skin had come away with his fingers, and for the first time in his life (in the world's life indeed, for before him no man had known it) he tasted – *crackling!* Again he felt and fumbled at the pig. It did not burn him so much now, still he licked his fingers from a sort of habit. The truth at length broke into his slow understanding, that it was the pig that smelt so, and the pig that tasted so delicious; and, surrendering himself up to the newborn pleasure, he fell to tearing up whole handfuls of the scorched skin with the flesh next it, and was cramming it down his throat when his father entered amid the smoking rafters, armed with retributory cudgel, and finding how affairs stood, began to rain blows upon the young rogue's shoulders, as thick as hailstones, which Bo-bo heeded not any more than if they had been flies. His father might lay on, but he could not beat him from his pig.

'You graceless whelp. Is it not enough that you have burnt down three houses with your dog's tricks, but you must be eating fire, and I know not what – what have you got there, I say?'

'O, father, the pig, the pig, do come and taste how nice the burnt pig is.'

The ears of Ho-ti tingled with horror. He cursed his son, and he cursed himself that ever he should beget a son that should eat burnt pig.

Bo-bo, whose scent was wonderfully sharpened since morning, soon raked out another pig, still shouting out 'Eat, eat, eat the burnt pig, father, only taste – O Lord.'

Ho-ti trembled in every joint while he grasped the abominable thing, wavering whether he should not put his son to death for an unnatural young monster, when the crackling scorching his fingers, as it had done his son's, and applying the same remedy to them, he in his turn tasted some of its flavour, which, make what sour mouths he would for a pretence, proved not altogether displeasing to him. In conclusion (for the manuscript here is a little tedious) both father and son promptly sat down to the meal, and never left off till they had despatched all that remained of the litter.

So, the discovery that the flesh of swine, or indeed of any other animal, might be cooked, was made.

(Adapted from A DISSERTATION UPON ROAST PIG: ESSAYS OF ELIA, Charles Lamb)

2   Ask the class for their critical comments. You could lead with the following questions:

   a   Do you think it is a true story? How can you tell?

   b   What caused the father to change his violent attitude to his 'graceless whelp' Bo-bo?

   c   Do you think that Charles Lamb enjoyed writing the story? What made you think so?

   d   Is roast pork your favourite 'roast'? or what?

3   Explain to the class that you are going to give them a name of something in our lives which is very common and which we often take for granted.
      Ask them to see if they can write a very short story (say 200 words) to explain its origin, and how it came to have its name. Here are some suggestions:

GROUP A	GROUP B	GROUP C
Reading glasses	A padlock	Language
A calendar	A calendar	A napkin ring
A table	Paper napkins	A calendar
Language	A comb	The wheel
The wheel	A clock	Gloves
Crisps	A fork	A ballpoint pen
A window frame	Cheese	Cornflakes
A doughnut	Trousers	An umbrella
An umbrella	An umbrella	A watch
A cupboard	Sunglasses	A shaver

4   The story of Charles Lamb's life is also worth telling: a remarkable story of a man's devotion to (and sacrifice for) his mentally sick sister; their initial poverty and their ultimate successes as writers and dramatists. In spite of all his personal troubles, Lamb still possessed a sense of humour, as the Roast Pig passage demonstrates.

35   FACT OR FABLE?   (Levels A, B & C)

This is an activity for individual work.

A fable can be described as a story in which creatures or inanimate objects act and speak like human beings, showing the same feelings and emotions as we do. It teaches us the difference between right and wrong, or how we ought to live our lives.

Listen to this fable which some of you may have heard before.

1   Read aloud:

Brer Rabbit, the Elephant and the Whale

'Yes,' said the elephant to Brer Rabbit, 'I don't think anyone would deny that I am the strongest creature on earth. Look how big I am.' And he drew himself up to his full height and raised his trunk in the air like a boxer who has just scored a knockout. 'I hope you don't think I'm boasting,' he went on. 'If you're as powerful as I am you can't help knowing it, any more than if you're a timid, feeble creature like you you can avoid knowing it.' He laughed unpleasantly.

Brer Rabbit laughed too, but he was not amused. 'My friend, don't be misled by your size,' he said. 'I know you can do a few party tricks like tearing up a tree by the roots, but you have no real strength – nothing to compare with my mighty muscles.' He sat up on his hind legs and drew in a deep breath to swell his tiny chest.

The elephant laughed so hard that he had to lean against a tree to save himself from falling. 'Your mighty muscles!' he choked. 'Oh dear, what a little comic you are!'

'I'm deadly serious,' said Brer Rabbit, 'and I'll prove it. Let's have a tug-o'-war. You take one end of this rope and I'll take the other. We'll see who can pull hardest.'

'This is ridiculous,' said the elephant, 'but I'll do it anyway. It'll teach you a lesson, you foolish little thing.'

Brer Rabbit tied the end of a long rope around the elephant's waist. 'Now I'll take the other end down on to the sands, through those bushes,' said Brer Rabbit. 'When I shout "Pull" do your worst.' The elephant agreed, Brer Rabbit tied the rope round him, and went off through the bushes on to the beach.

Not far out in the water a whale was sunning himself. 'Hello,' shouted Brer Rabbit, 'wasn't it you who told me yesterday that you were the strongest creature on earth?'

'It was,' answered the whale, 'but I don't suppose it was any news to you. I believe it's widely known.'

'I think I'm stronger than you,' said Brer Rabbit, 'and I'm ready to prove it. Let's have a tug-o'-war to see who's the tougher. I'll tie this rope around your waist and take the other end through the bushes up on to the grass. When I shout "Pull" pull. Okay?'

'Okay,' said the whale, hardly able to believe what he heard. Brer Rabbit tied the end of the rope round the great middle of the whale and went back up into the bushes. Once there he could not keep himself from laughing at the idea of the elephant at one end of the rope and the whale at the other. Then he shouted, 'Pull.'

The elephant gave a gentle tug. Nothing happened. He planted his great feet in the grass and gave a hefty pull. The whale was yanked his own length through the water.

'Cor!' he said, 'This little bloke isn't as feeble as he looks. I'll have to teach him a lesson.' With a powerful thrashing of his mighty tail he headed out to sea. The elephant found himself dragged off his feet and sliding along the grass on his bottom. He managed to slither to his feet and dug them into the ground to avoid being pulled into the sea. Then slowly he inched his way back from the bushes, where Brer Rabbit was lying chuckling at the groans and grunts of the two sweating giants. The whale felt himself slipping back towards the shore. He too exerted all his enormous strength. The great beasts strained at the rope until each was on the verge of collapse.

Brer Rabbit saw his chance. He shouted to the elephant, 'I could keep this up all day. Do you want to give up?'

'Yes,' gasped the elephant, falling gratefully on the grass.

Brer Rabbit turned towards the sea. 'Want to give up?' he shouted.

'I surrender,' panted the whale, as he sank to the bottom for a rest. As Brer Rabbit untied the rope from the defeated beasts he had the same message for each: 'Pride comes before a fall and boasting is always punished.'

(From: 101 SCHOOL ASSEMBLY STORIES: Carr)

2   Ask the pupils to comment on the story. You could lead with the following questions:

a   Do you think Brer Rabbit was wicked or right in what he did? Was his trickery justified?

b   Who do you think was the hero? Why?

c   Does the biggest or strongest person always win in life? Can you give other examples?

d   How effective was it to teach the lesson in this way? What will make you remember that 'pride comes before a fall'?

3   Now ask the pupils to see if they can write a fable to show people a truth in life.
They can either make up a fable using their own characters and choosing their own ideas about what they want to teach people, or they may choose one of the following suggestions:

CHARACTERS	LESSON
A cat and a mouse	Brains are better than brawn
A cat and a goldfish	Never trust a flatterer
A butterfly and a moth	Beauty is in the eye of the beholder
A bee and a rabbit	Save for the future
The grass and the oak tree	It is easier to go with others than against them
Fire, air, water and earth	We all have a part to play in life

36 DESCRIBING PLACES (Levels A, B & C)

'Describing places' is an exercise very like 'describing people'. It is easy to make a town or scene appear very ordinary rather than special and atmospheric. This exercise aims to help pupils realise that describing a scene needs not only the facts of its outward appearance; it also needs something about what it *feels like* to be there. Every place has the potential for exciting and interesting action.

The session should begin with a class exercise and then move to individual work.

1   With the whole class, as a board exercise, take the heading of THE CLASSROOM you are in. Draw up two lists of information that might be covered by a description of that room. List (a) should cover what it looks like; List (b) should cover what it is like to be in it, i.e. people's feelings about the place. You might cover such things as:

LIST (a)
1   Size/shape
2   Colour scheme. (Does it make you feel welcome; how does it affect your mood)
3   Something special about the room
4   What the windows look out onto
5   Decoration/work displayed on the walls

LIST (b)

1 Temperature (How does this affect the way you feel about the room?)
2 Atmosphere
3 Smells/noise
4 The mood of the class
5 Something memorable about the room

2 Now explain that as with descriptions of people, we must really try to make our descriptions sound interesting and memorable if we want others to feel that they are in our picture, so to speak.

Still with the whole class, compare the following descriptions. (You may wish to write these up on the board.)

1 (a) The pupils were working busily on their projects
  (b) The gentle drone from the groups working together soon became a buzz of excitement as the final design became clear.

2 (a) The desks were arranged in rows facing a white board
  (b) An army of desks, arranged in rows with military precision, faced an expectant whiteboard.

3 (a) It was a nice room
  (b) The room surrounded you with a sense of warmth and friendliness that promised a happy, dreamy last lesson.

Now see what descriptive phrases the class might offer you for the following:
1 My bedroom
2 A walk in the park on a winter's morning
3 The football stadium
4 On the river

3 Pupils should now work individually.
Write the following list of places on the board. You may add any other suggestions you wish. Ask the pupils to choose ONE and write a paragraph describing what it looks like and how it feels to be there.
1 The city at night
2 The street where you live
3 At the beach
4 A special place you like to visit/go to in your spare time

DEVELOPMENT

You might like to continue the exercise involving the descriptions of people and places, creating a descriptive composition.

The following are some suggested titles:

1   At the fair
2   My first day at . . .
3   At the concert/art gallery
4   Sunday at home
5   A foggy morning
6   The railway station

Shakespeare Shake-Out

Universal Themes

The purpose of this section is to try and focus on the universal themes and the human condition that are all so much part of Shakespeare's plays. Too often pupils feel daunted by the language and therefore afraid to tackle the words. These activities focus on some of the plays used in schools and seek to open them up by tackling parts of them in ways that pupils understand and from which they can gain enjoyment. If pupils can enjoy an exercise, they will be receptive to the purpose behind it and to the whole work.

37 LOVE AT NINNY'S TOMB: A Midsummer Night's Dream (Levels A, B & C)

This is an exercise for small groups which can be done (a) after reading the play or (b) beforehand. Shakespeare had a wonderful sense of fun. He enjoyed taking aspects of human life, like love and friendship, and making us laugh at how foolish we often look to others when we get carried away or take ourselves too seriously.

(a) *Set the Scene:* In A Midsummer Night's Dream, some artisans have been asked to put on some entertainment for a group of VIPs. They decide to act out a love story to entertain them, a choice which is particularly good as three couples in the group have just got married.

Explain to the pupils that they work for one of the TV production companies that produces programmes for the BBC. They have heard of the play put on by the artisan group and have decided it would make a good comedy programme for television.

In small groups, or pairs, ask the pupils to take the story of 'Ninny's Tomb' and draw up the storyboard for the TV production.

Remind them that their 'cartoon' should have all the action. They can add any words they feel might help the producer.

(b)   The same introduction can be given to the class but the teacher will need to give extra guidance to the pupils if the story is, as yet, unknown. The exercise can be carried out as a lead-in to the play within the play.

First, brainstorm with the pupils as a whole-class exercise, the essential ingredients of a love story. Careful guidance and questioning can bring out the outline of the Pyramus and Thisbe story.

> e.g. Think of an unusual place for lovers to meet.
> Give me two names for the boy and girl which are really different. (If nothing exciting comes up, offer Pyramus and Thisbe yourself – it usually sets the mood!)
> What do you think could attack and frighten the girl into running away – try something really unexpected. (I have actually been offered a *lion* at this point!)

Once this outline is on the board, the task of drawing up the programme storyboard can proceed as for section (a).

38   ROMEO AND JULIET: The Generation Gap (Levels A, B & C)

Romeo and Juliet would be able to relate to most modern teenagers who at some time or other find their parents unhappy with their actions or choice of partner. This exercise seeks to show how the feelings, anxieties and frustrations of parents and the younger generations in Shakespeare's time are still being played out today.

1   As a board exercise with the whole class, ask the pupils to brainstorm two lists:
    (a)   the reasons why parents might object to some girlfriend/boyfriend combinations;
    (b)   why it might be a good thing if these young people did come together.

Now, still with the whole class to help you, and using the play for reference if need be, go back over the lists and highlight the reasons that might apply to Romeo and Juliet.

2   Once step 1 has been completed, divide the class into pairs or small groups of three or four. Half the class should choose to work with Juliet and her family; the other half should choose to work with Romeo and his family.
     Set the scene as follows:
     The families are each at dinner and discussing the situation between Romeo and Juliet. Ask the pupils to write the dialogue which takes place at the family dinner tables.
     Care should be taken to accurately reflect the feelings of the two sides. How will the discussions end?

39   JULIUS CAESAR: For the History Books (Levels B & C)

Political life has its ups and downs with leaders gaining and losing the favour and esteem of fellow politicians for a variety of reasons.
   This exercise aims to examine Caesar's contribution to government as perceived by his contemporaries in the play.

1   Divide the class into small groups of three or four, half of whom should be asked to concentrate on Brutus's perceptions of Caesar, and the other half on Antony's views.
     The groups should spend some time brainstorming the arguments of their alloted persona as to how they would have Caesar recognised by history.

2   The second part of the lesson should be set up as a TV debate with a chair-person and two panels consisting of one representative of each of the 'Brutus' groups on one side, and one representative each of the 'Antony' groups on the other.
     The ensuing debate should attempt to determine how Caesar might be remembered in the history books.

There have been many times in the past when it has been vital for kings, queens, politicians and leaders of many different organisations to boost the morale of soldiers, political parties or teams to put them in the right frame of mind to win the day.

Queen Elizabeth I rallied her troops at Tilbury Docks when faced with the Spanish Armada threat; Winston Churchill made his famous "We'll fight them on the beaches" speech, and Henry V encouraged his tired troops with the St. Crispin's Day address (extracts from each are printed at the end of this unit).

This exercise aims to examine the ingredients which are common in all rallying calls.

1   As a class exercise, brainstorm the ideas that might be common in morale boosting addresses, regardless of century or purpose. Amongst others you might include such things as:

(a)   Common need/belief/brotherhood
(b)   Overcoming an opponent/difficulty
(c)   Personal/team/national honour
(d)   Repetition of important phrases

2   Still as a class exercise, ask the pupils to give you ideas for causes that might need a leader's speech to boost the morale of the 'troops', e.g. a political party rally, a school sports team about to play an important game, or a situation of local or national pride.

3   Divide the pupils into small groups of three or four. Ask each group to choose its cause and name the leader, and then write the rallying speech that might be given to those working for the cause. Care should be taken to use some of the ideas ascertained in step 1.

If there is time, each group might like to choose a spokesperson to 'deliver' the speech to the rest of the class.

4   Go back to Henry V's speech and examine with the class what ideas he incorporated into his rallying call.

Extract from Queen Elizabeth I's speech at Tilbury Docks, 1588
"My loving people, we have been persuaded by some that are careful

of our safety, to take heed how we commit ourselves to armed multitudes, for fear of treachery. But I assure you, I do not desire to live to distrust my faithful and loving people. Let tyrants fear. I have always so believed myself that, under God, I have placed my chiefest strength and safeguard in the loyal hearts and good will of my subjects; and therefore I am come amongst you, as you see, at this time, not for my recreation and disport, but being resolved, in the midst and heat of the battle, to live or die amongst you all, to lay down for my God, and for my kingdom, and for my people, my honour and my blood, even in the dust. I know I have the body of a weak and feeble woman, but I have the heart and stomach of a king, and a king of England too, and think foul scorn that Parma or Spain, or any Prince of Europe should dare to invade the borders of my realm; to which, rather than any dishonour shall grow by me, I myself will take up arms, I myself will be your general, judge and rewarder of every one of your virtues in the field. I know, already for your forwardness you have deserved rewards and crowns; and we do assure you, in the word of a prince, they shall be duly paid you."

Extract from Winston Churchill's speech, June 1940
We shall go on to the end, we shall fight in France, we shall fight on the seas and oceans, we shall fight with growing confidence and growing strength in the air, we shall defend our island, whatever the cost may be, we shall fight on the beaches, we shall fight on the landing grounds, we shall fight in the fields and in the streets, we shall fight in the hills; we shall never surrender.

Extract from Henry V: St. Crispin's Day Address
He which hath no stomach for this fight,
Let him depart; his passport shall be made,
And crowns for convey put into his purse:
We would not die in that man's company
That fears his fellowship to die with us.
This day is called the feast of Crispin:
He that outlives this day and comes safe home,
Will stand a tip-toe when this day is nam'd,
And rouse him at the name of Crispian.
He that shall live this day, and see old age
Will yearly on the vigil feast his neighbours,
And say, "Tomorrow is Saint Crispian's"

Then will he strip his sleeve and show his scars,
And say, "These wounds I had on Crispian's day."
Old men forget: yet all shall be forgot,
But he'll remember with advantages
What feats he did that day. Then shall our names,
Familiar in his mouth as household words,
Harry the King, Bedford and Exeter,
Warwick and Talbit, Salisbury and Gloucester,
Be in their flowing cups freshly remember'd.
This story shall the good man teach his son;
And Crispin Crispian shall ne'er go by,
From this day to the ending of the world,
But we in it shall be remembered;
We few, we happy few, we band of brothers;
For he today that sheds his blood with me
Shall be my brother; be he ne'er so vile
This day shall gentle his condition.
And gentlemen in England, now a-bed
Shall think themselves accurs'd they were not here,
And hold their manhoods cheap whiles any speaks
That fought with us upon Saint Crispin's day.

Miscellany

Classroom Quizzes

Quizzes are always useful to have on hand. They are entertaining as well as constructive ways of making pupils think about their language. The following examples could be used with classes, divided into teams or groups, offering correct answers to questions put by the teacher. (Dictionaries will be found helpful for most exercises.)

41 IDIOMS (Levels B & C)

In everyday speech we often use idioms wihout being aware of them and yet, when seen in written form, they can often seem ambiguous and misleading.

Explain the meaning of the following well-known idioms.

a   She made a waspish remark about him.

b   He hadn't seen them for donkey's years.

c   They chaired him off the field.

d   She left the job under a cloud.

e   He blamed the problems on red tape.

f   He was given the boot for throwing a spanner in the works.

g   They caught him red-handed.

h   He was feeling a little under the weather.

i   The news knocked him for six.

j   They couldn't see the wood for the trees.

k   She was very catty about his wife wearing the trousers.

l   He gave the talk off the cuff.

m   He was always going against the tide.

n   She was feeling extremely blue.

o   The black sheep of the family eventually found himself a plum job.

p   It's no good crying over spilt milk.

q   The problem was a thorny one.

r   She was very green when she started.

s   She had cold feet when she went for the interview.

t   He was told to stop talking through his hat.

u   He had them on the mat.

v   Everything was at sixes and sevens.

w   The manager was hand in glove with the directors.

x   She soon put a spoke in their wheel.

y   They were hoping to buttonhole the man in the corridor.

z   She was left out in the cold because she was wet.

42   FIFTY IMPOSSIBLE SPELLINGS!
(Levels B & C)

---

tortoise	dahlia
vaccinate	rhododendron
threshold	ecclesiastical

variegated	gnome
amnesia	liquefy
misshapen	battalion
paraffin	chrysalis
pneumonia	guttural
millennium	intrigue
magnanimous	saccharine
posthumous	sciatica
chlorophyll	rhapsody
dissension	criticism
hieroglyphics	broccoli
infinitesimal	labyrinth
loathsome	pseudonym
illicit	parasol
questionnaire	isosceles
anxiety	paraphernalia
fuchsia	philatelist
cyclamen	panicky
rebellion	rhetorical
vehemently	veterinary
valedictory	rendezvous
forty	pageant

43 SILENT LETTERS (Levels A, B & C)

There are a number of letters which form the spelling of words that are not actually sounded at all. This is one of the reasons why the

English language is so intriguing. Below are some examples. Ask the pupils to find as many as they can within a given time limit (say, 5 minutes).

silent B

Climb, crumb, debt, doubt, dumb, indebted, lamb, limb, numb, redoubt, subtle, thumb.

silent C

Abscess, abscind, indict, scene, scent, sceptre, science, scimitar, scissors, victuals.

silent CH

Schism.

silent G

Arraign, assign, campaign, consign, deign, design, ensign (which is accented on the first syllable), foreign, gnash, gnat, gnaw, gnome, gnostic, gnu, reign, resign, sign, sovereign.

silent GH

Blight, bright, bough, caught, delight, fight, flight, fright, height, high, light, might, naught, neighbour, nigh, night, ought, plight, plough, right, sigh, sight, slight, slough, straight, taught, thigh, tight, weight, wrought.

silent H

Heir, honest, honour, hour.

silent K

Knack, knapsack, knave, knead, knee, knew, knife, knight, knit, knob, knock, knoll, knot, knowledge, knuckle.

silent L

Balm, behalf, calf, calm, palm, psalm, salmon.

silent N

Autumn, column, condemn, hymn, solemn.

silent P

Corps, pneumatic, pneumonia, psalm, pseudo, psychic, pyschology, Ptolemy, receipt.

silent S

Island, isle, viscount.

silent UE

Catalogue, dialogue, epilogue, harangue, prologue, synagogue.

silent U

Colleague, guarantee, guard, guess, guest, plague, prologue, rogue, vague.

silent UGH

Although, bough, dough, nought, through.

silent W

Answer, sword, wrap, wreak, wreath, wreck, wren, wrench, wrestle, wretched, wriggle, wring, wrinkle, wrist, write, wrong.

44 FOREIGN PHRASES (Levels B & C)

We use many foreign phrases in our everyday lives. Do you know what the following mean?

faux pas	a mistake (social)
en masse	in a large number
à la carte	individually priced
à la mode	fashionable
ad lib	without planning
au fait	expert
bête noire	pet hate
bon voyage	a good journey
fait accompli	an accomplished fact
par excellence	of the highest order

carte blanche	freedom of action
coup d'etat	violent over-throwing of the government
blasé	unappreciative
impasse	a position from which there is no escape
laissez-faire	lack of government interference
nom de plume	pen name
rapport	relationship
tour de force	feat of skill or strength
nota bene	note well NB
post mortem	after death/after the event
status quo	the unchanged original position
debacle	collapse, downfall, disaster
et cetera	and so on
gourmet	one who appreciates the best in food and drink
hoi polloi	the multitude
genre	type

45 PLURALS (Levels A, B & C)

English has different ways of showing the plurals of nouns. Can you provide the correct form of the plurals for the following. It is suggested that a correct answer earns a half mark, the other half mark being awarded if the whole word is correctly spelled.

eskimo	–s	innuendo	–(e)s
concerto	i	criterion	a
echo	–es	radio	–s
cupful	–s†—	ratio	–s

diagnosis	es	casino	–s
bureau	–x	motto	–es
studio	–s	crisis	es
terminus	i	datum	a
bacterium	a	banjo	–s
handful	–s	solo	–s
cameo	–s	ass	–es
tomato	–es	cargo	–es
passer-by	–s-by	erratum	a
oasis	es	formula	ae/–s
half	ves	court-martial	–s-martial
roof	–s	spoonful	–sf–
son-in-law	s-in-law	belief	–s

46 ABBREVIATIONS (Levels A, B & C)

We live in an age where abbreviations have become everyday usage, particularly in newspapers. What do the following abbreviations stand for?

NATO	North Atlantic Treaty Organisation
UNO	United Nations Organisation
UFO	unidentified flying object
Hi-Fi	high fidelity
FBI	Federal Bureau of Investigation
EEC	European Economic Community
AA	Automobile Association

·RSVP	répondez s'il vous plait (reply, if you please)	
LED	light emitting diode	
TIR	Transports Internationaux Routiers (International Road Transport)	
HP	hire-purchase	(hp) horsepower
GMT	Greenwich Mean Time	
HGV	heavy goods vehicle	
LASER	light amplification by stimulated emission of radiation	
UNESCO	United Nations Educational, Scientific and Cultural Organisation	
USSR	Union of Soviet Socialist Republics	
VAT	Value Added Tax	
SAE	stamped, addressed envelope	
ETA	estimated time of arrival	
DJ	disc-jockey	

vet	veterinary surgeon	fab	fabulous
bus	omnibus	super	superlative
flu	influenza	perm	permanent wave
lunch	luncheon	cab	cabriolet
plane	aeroplane	fan	fanatic
phone	telephone	pops	popular tunes
cinema	cinematograph	fridge	refrigerator
exam	examination	mike	microphone
pub	public house	trad	traditional
zoo	zoological gardens	mod	modern

Explain what is wrong with the following sentences or statements for 1 mark. Suggest a better, clearer way of giving the information for a second mark.

a   Wanted: a man to wash dishes and two waitresses.

b   Funerals: parking for clients only.

c   Cheap Sponge Roll: take a teacupful of flour and mix it with a teaspoon of caster sugar and a teaspoonful of baking powder; break two eggs into a cup, then slide into the mixture.

d   Emma found herself on a stool by the nursery fire. Securely pierced by a long brass toasting fork she held a piece of bread to the glowing flameless fire.

e   The old duke picked up a snapshot of a dear friend who had recently died on his bedroom mantlepiece.

f   Notice to milkman: Baby arrived yesterday. Please leave another one.

g   From a Parish magazine: All those wishing to give eggs to the needy are asked to lay them in the font.

h   Dining table for sale by lady with Queen Anne legs.

i   His mother only guessed the cause of his anxiety.

j   Notice in a laundrette: Please remove your clothes as soon as all the lights are out.

k   You won't catch a cold walking in the fresh air.

l   Nobody has been in the library for more than 10 minutes.

Record of Units Used

DATE	CLASS	UNIT	LEVEL	NOTES

DATE	CLASS	UNIT	LEVEL	NOTES

DATE	CLASS	UNIT	LEVEL	NOTES